GRATITUDE JOURNAL

GRATITUDE
journal

JUDITH RUGGERI

GRATITUDE *journal*

JUDITH RUGGERI

Judith Ruggeri 2022

All materials contained in this book are the copyrighted property of Judith Ruggeri. To reproduce, publish, post, modify, distribute or display this publication You must first obtain permission from the author at:

Judith Ruggeri
5 Carlisle Street
Hamlyn Terrace
NSW 2259

Published by : Judith Ruggeri
Distributed by: Judith Ruggeri

ISBN: 978-0-646-86554-6

Writing, Editing & Design by Judith Ruggeri

Printed In Australia

ACKNOWLEDGEMENTS

I WOULD LIKE TO ACKNOWLEDGE
MY SISTER
SUSAN WAGSTAFF
FOR HER
ADVICE AND ASSISTANCE IN
BRINGING THIS JOURNAL TO
FRUITION.

PREFACE

A DAILY REMINDER OF THE GOODNESS OF GOD AND HOW BLESSED WE ARE REGARDLESS OF OUR CIRCUMSTANCES.

THIS JOURNAL CONTAINS PAGES WITH INSPIRATIONAL IDEAS TO GET YOU WRITING. PAGES WITH SCRIPTURES OF PRAISE AND GRATITUDE AND BLANK PAGES FOR YOU TO LET LOOSE WITH YOUR THOUGHTS AND IDEAS.

JAMES 1:17 NIV

EVERY GOOD AND PERFECT GIFT
IS FROM ABOVE, COMING DOWN
FROM THE FATHER OF THE
HEAVENLY LIGHTS,
WHO DOES NOT CHANGE
LIKE SHIFTING SHADOWS.

GRATITUDE CONTEMPLATION

I AM TRULY GRATEFUL FOR...

GRATITUDE PONDERING

WHAT THINGS DO YOU VALUE IN YOUR LIFE?

DATE:

MY NOTES

GRATITUDE TODAY

I AM INSPIRED TODAY TO DO THESE THINGS OUT OF GRATITUDE.

MY GRATITUDE LIST

ITEMISE THINGS YOU ARE GRATEFUL FOR.

DATE:

MY NOTES

DATE:

MY NOTES

GRATITUDE STUDY

HOW AM I FEELING TODAY?

WHAT POSITIVE THOUGHTS CAN I MEDITATE ON TODAY?

GRATITUDE OUTLOOK

TELL OF THE THINGS YOU ARE LOOKING FORWARD TO.

DATE:

MY NOTES

PHILLIPIANS 4:11

I HAVE LEARNED TO BE CONTENT IN WHATEVER STATE I AM.

GRATITUDE CONSIDERATION

TODAY I WILL LIST EVERYTHING I AM GRATEFUL FOR.

Draw or describe your home and how you feel about it.

DATE:

MY NOTES

DATE:

MY NOTES

GRATITUDE

LIST ALL THE THINGS I AM GRATEFUL FOR...

GRATITUDE LOG

LIST YOUR POSITIVE DECLARATIONS

DATE:

MY NOTES

BE KIND TO YOURSELF

DESCRIBE HOW YOU WILL SPOIL YOURSELF.

EXPECTATIONS

MY GOALS

WHY?

HOW

DATE:

MY NOTES

DATE:

MY NOTES

SELF-CARE

WHAT DO YOU PLAN TO DO...
TO LOOK AFTER YOU...

PHYSICAL

EMOTIONAL

SPIRITUAL

MENTAL

SOCIAL

ENVIRONMENTAL

GRATITUDE
LOVE

PEOPLE I LOVE

HOW CAN I BLESS THEM

REMINDER

SOLILOQUAY

DATE:

MY NOTES

EZRA 3:11 (NIV)

WITH PRAISE AND THANKSGIVING
THEY SANG TO THE LORD:

GRATEFUL

DATE:

DESCRIBE YOUR FAVOURITE TIME OF DAY & WHY.

_____
_____
_____
_____
_____
_____
_____
_____
_____
_____
_____
_____
_____
_____
_____
_____
_____
_____
_____

GRATEFUL
FOR ME

WHAT ARE YOUR PLANS FOR SELF-CARE

PHYSICAL	EMOTIONAL

SPIRITUAL	INTELLECTUAL

SOCIAL	ENVIRONMENTAL

DATE:

MY NOTES

DATE:

MY NOTES

Send a letter to a far away friend or relative.

GRATITUDE ACTIVITIES

LIST ALL THE ACTIVITIES THAT I LOVE AND AM GRATEFUL FOR.

E.G. MUSIC, SPORT, ART, SWIMMING, TENNIS

GRATITUDE

YOUR FAVOURITE MEAL

WHAT IS YOUR
FAVOURITE MEAL

WHO COOKED YOUR
FAVOURITE MEAL

HOW WILL YOU THANK
THIS PERSON

DATE:

MY NOTES

GRATITUDE
FRIENDS

FRIENDS YOU ARE GRATEFUL FOR

HAPPY MEMORIES WITH YOUR FRIENDS

WHAT IS YOUR FRIENDS NICEST QUALITY?

WHAT IS SOMETHING YOU CAN DO FOR YOUR FRIEND?

BE KIND TO OTHERS

DESCRIBE HOW YOU WILL SPOIL SOMEONE ELSE...

How can you help someone else today?

DATE:

MY NOTES

DATE:

MY NOTES

PSALM 50:23 ESV

THE ONE WHO OFFERS THANKSGIVING AS HIS SACRIFICE GLORIFIES ME; TO ONE WHO ORDERS HIS WAY RIGHTLY I WILL SHOW THE SALVATION OF GOD!

What is your favourite kind of food?

SELF-CARE

PHYSICAL

EMOTIONAL

WHAT DO YOU PLAN TO DO

SPIRITUAL

MENTAL

TO LOOK AFTER YOU...

SOCIAL

ENVIRONMENTAL

DATE:

MY NOTES

DATE:

MY NOTES

AURORA

GOOD MORNING MY FEELINGS TODAY ARE...
(HAPPY, SAD, OR EXCITED!)

I PRAY THE LORD WILL BLESS MY DAY
(INCLUDE FAVOURITE SCRIPTURE)

GRATITUDE

LIST ALL THE THINGS I AM
GRATEFUL FOR...

SOLILOQUAY

DATE:

MY NOTES

DATE:

MY NOTES

Who is someone new you have met recently that really made you feel happy?

SELF-CARE

WHAT DO YOU PLAN TO DO...

TO LOOK AFTER YOU...

PHYSICAL

EMOTIONAL

SPIRITUAL

MENTAL

SOCIAL

ENVIRONMENTAL

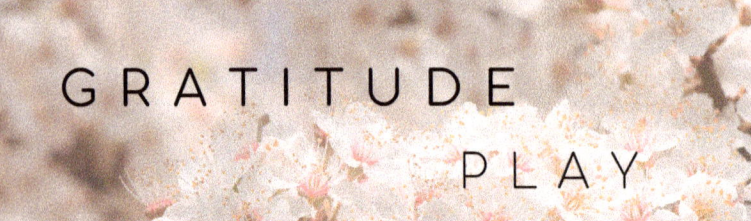

GRATITUDE PLAY

ENJOY YOUR DAYS UNDER THE SUN...
(ECCLESIASTES 9:9)

WHAT ARE YOU GOING TO DO TO PLAY TODAY?

DATE:

MY NOTES

DATE:

MY NOTES

S O L I L O Q U A Y

MATTHEW 6:21 NIV

FOR WHERE YOUR TREASURE IS,
THERE YOUR HEART WILL BE ALSO.

GRATITUDE CONTEMPLATION

TODAY WAS WONDERFUL BECAUSE...

WHAT NEW THINGS DID I DISCOVER TODAY...

DATE:

MY NOTES

DATE:

MY NOTES

AURORA

WHAT EXCITING THINGS HAVE I GOT PLANNED TODAY?

I PRAY THE LORD WILL BLESS MY DAY
(INCLUDE FAVOURITE SCRIPTURE)

if you were on a deserted island what three things would you take and why?

POSITIVE
MOTIVATION

FIRST PRIORITY

DATE:

MY NOTES

DATE:

MY NOTES

Journal about the person who blessed you recently and to whom you are grateful...

MY GRATITUDE LIST

ITEMISE THINGS YOU ARE GRATEFUL FOR.

GRATITUDE

DATE:

JOURNEY

PSALM 9:1 NIV

I WILL GIVE THANKS TO YOU, LORD,
WITH ALL MY HEART;
I WILL TELL OF ALL
YOUR WONDERFUL DEEDS.

Photos that I love. People, nature and things...

YOUR PHOTO
& STORY

DATE:

MY NOTES

DATE:

MY NOTES

GRATITUDE

APPRECIATION

DATE:

MY NOTES

DATE:

MY NOTES

GRATITUDE REFLECTION

REFLECT ON ALL THE WONDERFUL THINGS YOU HAVE BEEN BLESSED WITH..

GRATEFUL

DATE:

DESCRIBE YOUR FAVOURITE MUSICIAN & WHY.

GRATITUDE

THANKFULLNESS

DATE:

MY NOTES

DATE:

MY NOTES

GRATITUDE
KINDNESS

TODAY I WILL REMEMBER ALL THE KIND THINGS PEOPLE HAVE DONE FOR ME...

Write or draw the special quality that makes me myself.

GRATITUDE
GENEROSITY

LOOK AROUND YOU. CAN YOU BE GENEROUS TO SOMEONE TODAY & HOW?

DATE:

MY NOTES

DATE:

MY NOTES

A U R O R A

THIS IS MY PLANNING DAY- WHAT ARE MY PLANS?

GRATITUDE RECOGNITION

TELL ME SOME OF THE THINGS YOU LIKE ABOUT YOURSELF...

COLOSSIANS 4:6 NASB

LET YOUR SPEECH ALWAYS BE WITH GRACE, AS THOUGH SEASONED WITH SALT, SO THAT YOU WILL KNOW HOW YOU SHOULD RESPOND TO EACH PERSON.

DATE:

MY NOTES

DATE:

MY NOTES

GREATEST STRENGTHS

2 TIMOTHY 1:7

GOD DIDN'T GIVE ME A SPIRIT OF FEAR, BUT OF POWER, LOVE AND A SOUND MIND.

THINGS I'M THANKFUL FOR BEING ABLE TO DO:

GRATITUDE
PLEASING

WHAT THINGS ARE PLEASING TO YOU...

DATE:

MY NOTES

DATE:

MY NOTES

BOUNTIFUL BOWL OF THANKS

GRATITUDE

/ /

FAVOURITES

MOMENT OF THE DAY

THINGS TO DO

What is an outrageous thing you would like to do?

DATE:

MY NOTES

DATE:

MY NOTES

GRATITUDE
GIFTS

GIFTS THAT KEEP ON GIVING...

GRATITUDE
HELP

WHO HAS HELPED ME & WHAT DID THEY DO?

WHO CAN I HELP & WITH WHAT?

MY DREAMS

DATE:

MY NOTES

DATE:

MY NOTES

PHILLIPIANS 4:4

REJOICE IN THE LORD ALWAYS
AGAIN I SAY REJOICE!

GRATEFUL DATE:

DESCRIBE YOUR FAVOURITE SPORTSPERSON & WHY.

GRATITUDE
GENEROSITY

IN YOUR LIFE WHO HAS BEEN
GENEROUS TO YOU...

DATE:

MY NOTES

DATE:

MY NOTES

MY GRATITUDE LIST

ITEMISE THINGS YOU ARE GRATEFUL FOR.

Is there a person who has had a big influence on your life?

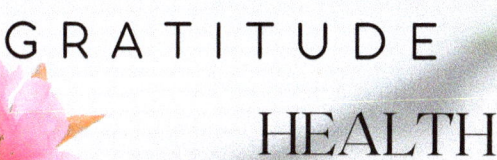

GRATITUDE
HEALTH

HOW IS YOUR HEALTH & WHAT ARE YOU DOING TO TAKE CARE OF IT?

DATE:

MY NOTES

GRATITUDE

TODAY I'M GRATEFUL FOR

GRATITUDE

TODAY, I'M GRATEFUL FOR...

DATE:

MY NOTES

DATE:

MY NOTES

NEHEMIAH 8:10

THE JOY OF THE LORD IS YOUR STRENGTH..

A U R O R A

ARISE & SHINE THE DAY IS BREAKING & YOU HAVE MUCH TO BE GRATEUL FOR……

DATE:

MY NOTES

GRATITUDE REFLECTION

MENTION THE THINGS YOU ARE LOOKING FORWARD TO

DATE:

MY NOTES

DATE:

MY NOTES

GRATITUDE
PEOPLE

LIST ALL THE PEOPLE IN YOUR LIFE THAT YOU ARE GRATEFUL FOR...

BOUNTIFUL BOWL OF THANKS

DATE:

MY NOTES

GRATITUDE FOR TODAY

THINGS I'M GRATEFUL FOR

GRATITUDE

ACTIVITIES

LIST SOME ACTIVITIES

YOU ENJOY

PSALM 118:24

THIS IS THE DAY THAT THE LORD
HAS MADE; WE WILL REJOICE
AND BE GLAD IN IT.

DATE:

MY NOTES

MY NOTES

GRATITUDE
WONDERFUL

WHAT ARE SOME OF THE WONDERS IN THIS WORLD

WRITE, DRAW OR PASTE PHOTOS OF ALL THE WONDERFUL THINGS IN YOUR LIFE.

TODAY I AM GRATEFUL FOR...

POSITIVE PROVISION

GRATITUDE SURPRISES

SOME PLEASANT SURPRISES I AM GRATEFUL FOR

DATE:

MY NOTES

GRATITUDE
GRACE

BY THE GRACE OF GOD

I AM

I HAVE

MY DREAMS

DATE:

MY NOTES

DATE:

MY NOTES

Are you happy with your body and looks?

GRATITUDE

PRAISE

FOR MY LIFE

MYSELF

PEOPLE THAT MATTER TO ME

WHO GIVES ME COMFORT?

HAPPY MEMORIES

JOY

GREATEST STRENGTHS

PSALM 139:14

I WILL PRAISE YOU, FOR I AM FEARFULLY AND WONDERFULLY MADE.

THINGS I'M THANKFUL FOR BEING ABLE TO DO:

DATE:

MY NOTES

PSALM 136 NIV

GIVE THANKS TO THE LORD,
FOR HE IS GOOD.
HIS LOVE ENDURES FOREVER.

With Gratitude

www.ingramcontent.com/pod-product-compliance
Lightning Source LLC
Chambersburg PA
CBHW040741020526
44107CB00084B/2836